LOOKING BACK AT BRITISH TUGS

by
Andrew Wiltshire

The **North End** was delivered to Alexandra Towing in June 1957 as the final unit of five similar tugs built in 1956/57. They were known locally by the Mersey tug crews as the "North boats". She was the odd one out being a product of W.J. Yarwood's shipyard at Northwich in Cheshire. The **North End** was 215 grt and measured 104 feet in length by 28 feet in the beam. Apart from a few minor detail differences she was the same as her sisters, all of which were oil fired. She had a triple expansion steam engine of 1050ihp built by Charles D. Holmes of Hull. As such she spent her entire working life based at Liverpool. Upon being sold in 1972 to new owners on the Italian island of Sardinia, she gained the name **Figari**. This was changed to **Bitti** in 1975 for her remaining years of service at port of Cagliari. It is not sure when she was finally taken out of use, although she was a stripped hulk by 1998. We see her here at work in the Liverpool dock system on 17 June 1971.

(Paul Boot)

Introduction

It all began back in the summer of 1966 when I was just five! I watched the steam tug **Ocean Cock** returning to her berth in the old dock basin at Felixstowe. It struck a chord. Upon returning to South Wales to live a few months later, weekend visits to Cardiff, Barry and Newport docks became the norm. The tugs became an instant fascination, especially those at Newport. In subsequent years my interest in tugs was bolstered with encouragement from the late Des Harris and from friend and tug skipper Danny Lynch.

In the early 1950s there were still many shipyards around the coast of the British Isles constructing motor tugs and even a few steam powered tugs. Commercially active steam tugs finally disappeared in the early 1980s, but there still remained great variety in the numerous tug fleets to be found around the UK. Tug design in the British fleets has evolved a great deal in the last 50 years and continues to do so. Until the 1960s, British tugs were both traditional in appearance and had conventional propulsion. Today, most new tugs are built overseas to standard designs and are quite technologically advanced.

The tug is very much a workhorse and the heart of the vessel is its power plant and its propulsion system. Traditionally the output of older steam tugs was recorded as either Nominal horse power (nhp) or more commonly in recent years Indicated horse power (ihp). That of motor tugs is usually shown as Brake horse power (bhp). An alternative to the conventional screw propeller appeared in the 1930s with the Voith Schneider cycloidal propulsion system. Further propulsion systems appeared in the 1970s and included the forward mounted Schottel units and stern drive Z-Peller and Aquamaster azimuthing units. Today we also have many variations of the above.

Looking back at British Tugs, takes a look at a variety of tugs used around the UK since the 1960s until the early 1990s. Sadly most of the companies and liveries featured in this book are now consigned to history and are just memories.

Acknowledgements

Once again a big thank you goes out to the many photographers who have made their work available for use in this book. Without their kind co-operation the book would not have that special quality to it. A special thanks also to my father John Wiltshire who has also promised to keep me supplied with more material for future projects!

A very big thank you must go to my good friend Kevin Blair who has once again helped enormously. He has proof read my scripts and researched certain facts and figures where I have drawn a blank. Thanks also to my friend and colleague Pete Brabham who has used his skills to help breathe new life into a couple of transparencies that were showing signs of ageing. Many thanks also to Bernard McCall for his help and guidance. Also to the newsgroup Tugtalk which has enabled further facts to be established. Written sources used throughout include various volumes of *Lloyd's Register of Shipping, Cory Towage* (by W.J. Harvey), *Empire Tugs* (by W.J. Harvey and K. Turrell), *Red Funnel and Before* (by R.B. Adams), *Fifty Years of Naval Tugs* (by Bill Hannan), *150 Years of the Maltese Cross* (by J.H. Proud), *Seahorses of the Tees* (by J.H. Proud) and *Blow Five* (by WB Hallam). Finally, my thanks go to Gil Mayes for once again checking the manuscript and to the Amadeus Press for their contribution to the finished book.

Andrew Wiltshire   Cardiff, July 2007

Published by Bernard McCall, 400 Nore Road, Portishead, Bristol, BS20 8EZ, England. Website : www.coastalshipping.co.uk
Telephone/fax : 01275 846178. E-mail : bernard@coastalshipping.co.uk
All distribution enquiries should be addressed to the publisher.

Printed by Amadeus Press, Ezra House, West 26 Business Park, Cleckheaton, West Yorkshire, BD19 4TQ
Telephone : 01274 863210; fax : 01274 863211; e-mail : info@amadeuspress.co.uk; website : www.amadeuspress.co.uk

ISBN : 978-1-902953-28-1

Front cover: The **Sea Alarm** was a member of the Warrior class of Empire Tug. She was one of four tugs built by J Crown of Sunderland, a builder not usually associated with constructing tugs. She was completed as the **Empire Ash** on 17 October 1941, had a gross tonnage of 263 and a 1000ihp triple expansion engine by Swan, Hunter and Wigham Richardson. She passed to the Clyde Shipping Co in 1946 and became the **Flying Fulmar**. Exactly 10 years later she was bought by C J King & Sons of Bristol. Renamed **Sea Alarm** she joined the **Sea Queen** (see page 17) working out of Avonmouth. Being a coal burner, in later years she was kept as the spare tug in the King fleet, and would periodically visit Barry in South Wales to replenish her coal bunkers. The **Sea Alarm** put in 16 years service before being retired. In January 1973 she was sold to shipbreaker T Ward and towed to Briton Ferry. The following month she was purchased by the National Museum of Wales for preservation and moved to Cardiff. She survived as an exhibit at the Industrial and Maritime Museum until June 1998 when she was broken up to make way for a new development. A great shame…..

(John Wiltshire)

Back cover: The 1961 built **Forager** passes Dumbarton Castle and heads downstream in the morning sunshine of 27 August 1976. She was completed for Steel and Bennie Ltd, of Glasgow, as the **Brigadier** at the yard of George Brown & Company of Greenock. As a Clyde based tug she would be responsible for ship handling at the various docks on the Upper Clyde as well as assisting at the numerous shipyards once found on the river. In 1969 Steel and Bennie became part of R & J.H. Rea and in 1970 passed to Cory Ship Towage. The **Brigadier** was given the name **Forager** in 1976, thus allowing her old name to be used on a brand new tug. She left Cory ownership later in 1976, and had a more modern wheelhouse fitted by her new owner Whitcliff Corporation (A & N Vogel Ltd), of London. Renamed **Fortrose** she was eventually resold for a new life in Italy in 1978. As far as is known, she was still working out of Naples in 2005.

(Nigel Jones)

The **Britonia** has to be one of the most attractive British-built motor salvage tugs. She was completed in 1963 at Appledore for the Overseas Towage & Salvage Co Ltd, of London. Her lines are a little reminiscent of some Dutch ocean-going salvage tugs of the 1950s and 1960s. The **Britonia** is a compact tug of 568 grt and is powered by a single 8-cylinder British Polar diesel with an output of 1680bhp. Her towing career was brief as in 1971 she was sold to Decca Surveys Ltd and converted for use as a survey ship. As such she was renamed **Decca Surveyor**. She later became **Bon Entente** owned by J. Mackee, of London, and is now owned by Aquatec Diving Services Ltd, Tema, Ghana. Here she makes a fine sight as she passes along the New Waterway in July 1971.

(Andrew Wiltshire collection)

The principal tug operator on the Medway for decades was J P Knight Ltd, of Rochester. However, this was to change in 1991 when they sold their Medway operations to the Howard Smith Group. Knight would then concentrate towage interests on their Scottish based fleet at Invergordon and in Surinam. The **Knighton** was a modern and powerful tug built in 1968 by Richards Shipbuilders, of Lowestoft. At 113 feet overall length and 276 grt she was quite a hefty-looking vessel. The **Knighton** had a 6-cylinder Mirrlees National main engine with an impressive output of 1810bhp which was powerful for a 1968 era harbour tug. This view dating from 30 April 1988 shows her attending to a reefer at Sheerness. Also in view is the similar **Kennet** of 1965. Instantly recognisable trade marks of the J P Knight fleet were the brown superstructure, distinctive funnel marking, and application of red paint to the lower hull above the waterline. After a number of years in the colours of Howard Smith Towage, the **Knighton** was sold in 2000 to LUTAMAR of Portugal and renamed **Resistente**.

(Andrew Wiltshire)

Upon withdrawal from service with London Tugs Ltd on the Thames in 1972, the *Cervia* was sold to the Medway Maritime Museum Society. A year later she was working commercially and operated by I.T.L (International Towing Ltd), of Sittingbourne. She remained active in this role until 1977. Completed in April 1946 as the **Empire Raymond** by A Hall, of Aberdeen, she became the *Cervia* later that year for William Watkins Ltd, of London. Tragically she capsized and sank in October 1954 while attending the passenger ship **Arcadia**, with the loss of five lives. Refloated and renovated, the *Cervia* went on to become an icon amongst Thames steam tugs and is a popular subject for modellers. Here she is seen at Newport towing away the redundant floating crane *GWR 30* in July 1975, whilst sailing for I.T.L. After a number years in lay up, she was sold to the East Kent Maritime Museum in 1983 for preservation at Ramsgate. Now restored she is still on display there in 2007.

(Danny Lynch)

The existence of a port at Dover can be traced as far back as Roman times. but it was not granted a Royal Charter until 1606. Being primarily a ferry port, ship towage at Dover has always been on a small scale. In the late 1950s the two remaining Harbour Board steam tugs were replaced by a pair of twin-screw motor tugs, the **Diligent** and **Dominant**. The **Diligent** was delivered in 1957 followed in 1958 by her sister. They were modern vessels for their time with twin exhaust uptakes in place of a funnel. The **Dominant** was built by P K Harris at Appledore, and had an output of 1040bhp giving a bollard pull of just over 16 tonnes. She is seen here in June 1978 looking very well cared for at 20 years of age. Both tugs were sold in 1984 to Frank Pearce (Tugs) Ltd, of Poole. The **Dominant** was then sold to Oil Transport Inc, of Miami, for further service in the Caribbean. Renamed **Kenneth**, she was put to work at Curacao and was last noted sailing as such in 1996.

(Andrew Wiltshire collection)

For 1984 delivery, the Dover Harbour Board had ordered two "twin unit" Voith-Schneider tractor tugs from McTay Marine Ltd at Bromborough on Merseyside. The new vessels were named **Deft** and **Dextrous** and were turned out with blue hulls and yellow funnels; they looked impressive. They were impressive performers too with a bollard pull of 29 tonnes provided by a pair of Ruston diesels. As well as handling cargo vessels at the Eastern Docks they would be called upon to assist the large ferries on and off the berths in strong winds. The opening of the new Cruise Ship Terminal at the Western Docks in the late 1990s attracted even larger ships to the port and more powerful tugs were needed. The existing tugs were therefore replaced in 2000 by two new stern drive tugs of greater bollard pull. The **Dextrous** is seen here in June 1999 crossing the harbour towards the Eastern Docks and the ferry terminals. The **Dextrous** passed to Howard Smith Towage for use on the Thames as the **Cobham**, the **Deft** becoming the **Shorne**.

(Bernard McCall)

In 1194, during the reign of King Richard 1 it was agreed to establish a Naval Base at Portsmouth. It grew as the centuries passed and became a busy port by the turn of the twentieth century. The tug fleet required to serve this facility was at one time quite substantial. The Admiralty had five Confiance Class tugs. This was originally a speculative venture by shipbuilder A & J Inglis, the design being taken over by the MoD. The **Agile** was completed in 1959 with pennant number A88 and was the only member of the class built by the Goole Shipbuilding Co. She was a twin-screw tug and each propeller shaft was driven by a pair of Paxman diesels. As such she had a free sea speed of 13 knots. Her career began based at Portsmouth but she did a spell as a Royal Fleet Auxiliary tug at Singapore from 1965 to 1967. She returned to the UK towing the **Frosty** to Rosyth but ended her days stationed at Gibraltar and was eventually sunk as a target in 1985. She is seen here at Portsmouth on 6 August 1974 in the company of the unique Type 82 destroyer **HMS Bristol**.

(C C Beazley)

Built mainly to work under the sponsons of aircraft carriers, the Director Class paddle tugs numbered seven in total. These were very unusual and quite impressive looking naval tugs. The *Griper* seen here was the last to be completed, in 1958. She was built on the Clyde by Wm Simons, of Renfrew. Her paddle wheels were independently driven by electric motors which made her very responsive and popular with crews. Power for each motor was provided by a pair of 12-cylinder Paxman diesels driving an electric generator. She had a massive 60 feet beam overall and had a full complement of 22 crew. The *Griper* was initially based at Rosyth but moved to Portsmouth in 1966 to join her sister, the *Grinder.* She was withdrawn in 1979 and sold to H G Pounds, before passing to a breaker at Gijon in northern Spain the following year. In this July 1977 view, the *Griper* can be seen performing a hard turn, and throwing water out through her paddle box apertures.

(Bob Allen)

Operating a fleet of tugs and ferries in the Solent, the Southampton, Isle of Wight and South of England Royal Mail Steam Packet Co Ltd was better known as Red Funnel. In 1953 the company took delivery of the locally-built **Hamtun** and **Sir Bevois** which would be their last steam tugs. Unlike earlier steam tugs this pair was built with oil-fired boilers. The **Sir Bevois** seen here, takes its name from a great local Saxon chief who was also a saviour of English Christianity. The previous tug of this name was sunk by enemy action during the Second World War. The **Sir Bevois** was 317 tons gross and had a pair of triple expansion engines totalling 1500ihp, driving twin propellers. This view of her underway on Southampton Water in August 1967 shows her extensive superstructure and the distinctive Thornycroft cowl on top of her funnel. In 1968 she was sold to contractor Howard Doris of Liverpool and renamed **Amanda Howard**. She received a major refit in 1971 but was sold two years later to Jack Martin of Dublin. Sadly in 1974 she was broken up in Ireland, as being an uneconomic proposition because of the increasing cost of bunker fuel.

(Danny Lynch)

Tender tugs had been part of the towage scene at Southampton for many years. The **Calshot** was to be the last tug/tender to operate at the port. She was delivered a little late in the day as work for tenders by the mid-1960s was diminishing. She was delivered in 1964 as a replacement for the steam-powered **Calshot** of 1930. She closely followed the design of the **Gatcombe** of 1960. However, she did have a fully-enclosed bridge and a differently-shaped funnel. Built locally by Thornycroft, the **Calshot** was 515 gross tons, twin-screw and of 2000bhp. She was certified to carry 215 pasengers. As tender work declined, the **Gatcombe** was sold in 1970. Following a solution to crewing problems, the

Calshot continued to work but as a tug, with occasional passenger duties. Another role for her was as an oil-dispersant vessel, which resulted in her travelling far and wide around the United Kingdom. She was kept in immaculate condition right up to her withdrawal in 1985 when she was replaced by the new tractor tug **Sir Bevois**. The **Calshot** was the last tender tug in the British Isles and had been sold by 1986 to owners in the Irish Republic via Havelet Services Ltd, of Totnes. Since 1992 she could be found sailing as the **Boluda Abrego** at Valencia in Spain.

(Andrew Wiltshire)

The other major tug operator at Southampton was the Alexandra Towing Company which had based tugs at the port for many years. In the 1960s it was found necessary to keep a smaller tug in the fleet, and initially this was a role performed by the former TID tug **Ower**. By 1979 the Thames tug **Sun XXIV** of 1962 had been transferred here. The **Sun XXIV** was built for W H J Alexander (Sun Tugs), of London, by J Pollock at Faversham. She was a conventional single-screw motor tug with a 720bhp Mirrlees oil engine. Sun Tugs became part of London Tugs Ltd in 1969. Then in 1975 London Tugs was taken over by Alexandra Towing. The **Sun XXIV**, seen here in April 1990, was sold later in the year to Subsearch Marine Services, a Newhaven contractor and went on to have a varied and sometimes dubious career. She still sails in 2007, undertaking mainly coastal contracts as the **Kingston** of Griffin Towage.

(Bernard McCall)

During the later years of the Second World War, the Admiralty specified a new design for a small dockyard tug. It was to be constructed with an all-welded steel hull and steam power plant. Known as "TIDs", they were constructed at just two yards. The **Bonchurch** was built as **TID 174** in 1944 by Dunstons at Thorne. The TID design was 74 feet in length by 18 feet in the beam and 53 gross tons. As **TID 174** she passed from Naval service to French owners in 1946 and later became the **Abeille No.13** in 1948. She arrived back in the UK in 1966 as the **Baie Comeau** after a brief spell with another French owner. She was re-engined and rebuilt at Bitterne along with a similar vessel. This took her tonnage up to 63 tons. Her life on the Solent began in the same year when Red Funnel bought her to ward off competition from Husbands Shipyard. Husbands operated a number of small tugs in the Southampton area. She gained the local name **Bonchurch**. She is seen here underway and heading towards Southampton on 10 April 1971. Only her hull gives a clue to her origin. Sold in 1983 she had a string of UK owners before being sold to an American buyer in 1998. He failed to take delivery of her, and after several further owners, turned up at Runcorn for sale in 2006.

(Nigel Jones)

There has been an oil refinery on the Solent at Fawley since 1921. It was rebuilt and enlarged by Esso Petroleum in 1951, and has gone on to become the largest refinery in the United Kingdom. To handle large tankers at the oil jetties Red Funnel deployed a number of tugs over the years, some with fire-fighting capabilities. Red Funnel was looking for a second generation of tugs to fill this role, but the usual supplier J I Thornycroft was no longer able to build commercial vessels. And so Red Funnel turned to Richard Dunston Ltd to supply two purpose-built firefighting tugs. They were delivered in November and December 1970 respectively. The pair took the traditional local names of **Gatcombe** and **Vecta** and were powerful single-screw tugs. Both had a 6-cylinder Mirrlees Blackstone

engine of 2500bhp and were fitted with a Kort-Nozzle giving a 35 tonne bollard pull. Perhaps the most unusual feature was the Simon Snorkel hydraulic firefighting platform mounted on top of the wheelhouse and they were also equipped with a portable boom for oil dispersal spraying. They are seen moored together at Fawley on 15 July 1983. Both tugs continued to serve at Fawley until 1994, when the contract was awarded to another towage operator. Both **Gatcombe** and **Vecta** have remained together as a pair in the Multraship fleet based at Terneuzen in the Netherlands. They now carry the names **Multratug 6** and **Multratug 8** respectively.

(Andrew Wiltshire)

The small Cornish china clay exporting port of Fowey has for years maintained a pair of ship-handling tugs. Fowey is located on the banks of the River Fowey on Cornwall's south coast, and is a natural deepwater harbour with a number of wharves. The **Gribbin Head** served at the port from 1968 until 1988. She started life as the **Ingleby Cross** in 1955 working for Tees Towing of Middlesbrough. She was built on the Clyde by Scott and Sons, of Bowling, and was one of three similar tugs. She had a 4-cylinder Crossley engine of 750bhp. The **Gribbin Head** was sold by the Fowey Harbour Commissioners after a major engine failure in 1988. Her new owners Haven Marine Services fitted a new English Electric power unit. She then passed via West Coast Towing to the Tuskar Rock Diving Co at Rosslare, Eire, and was renamed **Tuskar Rock**. In 1996 she was sold to Pinturas at Huelva in Spain and is believed to still be in service in 2007 as **Tuskar Rock**.

(Bernard McCall)

13

Falmouth had the distinction of being the last port in the British Isles to host regular steam tug operation. The **St. Merryn**, shown here on 17 September 1980, was one of the last two examples in action. She was similar in size to an Empire tug (233 grt and 1000ihp), but was in fact ordered by the Admiralty although paid for and built under the direction of the Canadian Government. Launched as the **Rock Pigeon**, she was built in 1945 by the Canadian Shipbuilding Co, of Ontario. She was put to work at Hong Kong and later Singapore where she was renamed **Flaunt** in 1948. She was purchased by the Falmouth Towage Co in 1959 and given the local name **St. Merryn**. Falmouth was not a commercial port in the true sense. It was largely a ship repair facility with several dry docks. Tugs would often be required to perform dead ship moves between drydock and berths. Another local feature was to provide fresh water and stores to any of the vessels laid up in the nearby River Fal. The **St. Merryn** was sold to a Dutch shipbreaker in 1984, having been replaced by a motor tug.

(Danny Lynch)

The Falmouth tug **St. Eval** still retains her classic lines and it is no surprise to learn that she was built way back in 1930. She started life as a steam tug, having been constructed as the **Chieftain** for Steel & Bennie Ltd, of Glasgow. Completed by Scott & Sons, Bowling, she had her steam machinery removed in 1957. In place of this appeared a Deutz diesel. Her life on the Clyde ended in 1967 when Falmouth Towage bought her to replace a steam tug. At this point she was re-engined once again. This time she received a 16-cylinder General Motors power unit of 858bhp. The **St. Eval** served Falmouth until 1987, when she was sold to businessman Peter de Savary for conversion into a tender to his racing yacht **Blue Arrow**. She still survives to this day as a private yacht based in the United States. She is seen on 2 February 1976 on the lower reaches of the River Fal and has a tanker in tow.

(Krispen Atkinson)

St. Gluvias was acquired in 1980 from Cory Ship Towage (via shipbreaker H Pound), as the **Cruiser**, with what is believed to have been stern tube damage. She was subsequently repaired and put to work at Falmouth. Built in 1959 by T Mitchison at Gateshead as the **Clonmel**, she was one of a pair of tugs ordered by J Cooper, of Belfast, and exemplifies the hydroconic hull design. Along with her sister, the **Cashel**, she was built specifically for use at the new Esso refinery at Whitegate in the Republic of Ireland, and registered at Cork. The **St. Gluvias** was fitted for firefighting and had a 6-cylinder Polar engine of 1260bhp driving a controllable pitch propeller. As part of the four-strong Falmouth Towage fleet, she is seen here demonstrating her fire monitors on 20 May 1986. Following disposal in 2001 she was under the ownership of Spithead Trading by 2006. In 2007, she was being refurbished at Lowestoft.

(Roy Cressey)

Modernisation of R & J H Rea's Bristol fleet began in 1959 when it was announced that a pair of motor tugs had been ordered from W J Yarwood & Sons, at Northwich. They would be modern-looking harbour tugs with Ruston & Hornsby oil engines of 870bhp and conventional single screws, giving a bollard pull of 13.6 tonnes. Other features would include a flying bridge, so that all operations could be conducted from this elevated position if required. The **Plumgarth** was delivered in February 1960 followed in June by the **Avongarth**. Whilst the **Plumgarth** moved across to the Cardiff and Barry fleet in 1961, the **Avongarth** was to remain on the English side of the Bristol Channel until 1979. She is seen here in Rea colours drifting along off Portishead in February 1967. The **Avongarth** passed to Cory Ship Towage in 1970 and she changed to their black and white colour scheme. She was eventually transferred to the Plymouth-based operation in 1979 where she joined the **Plumgarth** once again. Ten years later in November 1989, Cory sold her to Holt Associates International Ltd, of Totnes, who renamed her **Tiverton**. She then moved on to find a new home working in Portugal as the **Galito**. She was broken up at Lisbon in 2005 as the **S. Vicente** of LUTAMAR.

(Derek Chaplin)

The **Sea Queen** was a Birch Class Empire tug built during the Second World War for the Ministry of War Transport. She was completed in 1944 as the **Empire Walter** and purchased by C J King & Sons, of Bristol, in 1946. Her owners had a pair of Empire tugs by 1956 but they were quite different in appearance. The **Sea Queen** was an oil-fired steam tug, unlike the coal-burning **Sea Alarm** (see front cover). Consequently in later years she was the favoured steam tug in use at Avonmouth. She would invariably be put to work as the "bow tug", as seen here on 19 May 1968 with a Stag Line cargo vessel in tow. Interesting points to note are the cowl to the top of her funnel and the tripod main mast. After 27 years service with C J King, she was withdrawn in 1973 and laid up at Avonmouth. After a failed preservation attempt, she was sold to breakers in northern Spain in 1974.

(John Wiltshire)

The **Sea Endeavour** is seen making a hasty departure from Avonmouth on 7 June 1982, with the Royal Portbury Dock in the background. She would be the last tug to be purchased by C J King & Son for use at Avonmouth and Portbury. Delivered on 31 August 1980, the **Sea Endeavour** was a very conventional but powerful single screw tug of 3150bhp and bollard pull of 42 tonnes. She was built by Richards Shipbuilders, of Great Yarmouth. Her lines were similar to, but more angular than, the earlier **Sea Challenge** of 1968. It is known that her Ruston main engine had reliability problems early in her career, but it is thought these were resolved. Kings sold their towage interests to Cory Ship Towage in 1983 and a new subsidiary, Cory King Towage, was set up. The **Sea Endeavour** gained the Cory Towage house colours in the late 1980s. The Cory business passed to Wijsmuller Marine in 2001 and later to Svitzer Marine. The **Sea Endeavour** soon became a spare tug and was sold to Saga Shipping in 2005 for use in the Caribbean and US Gulf. As of September 2006 she had failed to leave Europe, and was laid up at Esbjerg.

(Danny Lynch)

A new oil refinery and terminal at Come-by-Chance in Newfoundland, Canada, required new four new firefighting tugs. In anticipation of this, a joint venture was set up between Cory Towage and Dutch tug operator Smit. The contract was won by Smit and Cory International, and was later increased to six tugs. The new tugs were to be built in the UK. The **Point Gilbert** was one of a pair delivered in 1972 by Richard Dunston. Powered by a 12-cylinder English Electric diesel with an output of 2640bhp, she had a bollard pull of 37 tonnes. She closely followed the design of the three G class tugs built in 1970 for Milford Haven. The refinery closed

after a few years, and by 1980 both **Point Gilbert** and sister ship **Point James** had returned to the UK. They were allocated to Avonmouth as more powerful tugs were now needed to work at Royal Portbury Dock. She makes a fine sight underway on 20 July 1980. In 1988 the **Point Gilbert** was fitted with a retractable Aquamaster bow unit, which increased her bollard pull to 45 tonnes. Passing to Wijsmuller in 2001, she was later transferred to the Clyde. She was sold in 2005 to Turquoise Holdings in the Netherlands and was offered for sale in 2006.

(Danny Lynch)

The **Lowgarth** was a further development of the **Avongarth**, and was to be the fifth new motor tug delivered to R & J H Rea for use in the upper Bristol Channel. Constructed by Richards Shipbuilders, of Lowestoft, she was delivered to the Cardiff fleet in March 1965. Her design would be evaluated pending a decision on ordering further motor tugs of similar size. She had a 7-cylinder Ruston & Hornsby engine giving 920bhp and driving a fixed pitch propeller in a steerable Kort-Nozzle. The **Lowgarth** worked at Cardiff and Barry until 1979 when she was moved across to Avonmouth. She put in a further 18 years service here, often being the preferred tug for use on the River Avon and up to Sharpness. She was sold in 1997 for use as a leisure facility on the River Weaver. The **Lowgarth** was, however, deemed unsuitable for this role and was sold to Rigg Shipping, of Ipswich, in September 2001. She was later renovated to a high standard at the Suffolk port, and in 2006 she was reported to be up for sale. The **Lowgarth** is depicted underway in Avonmouth docks in June 1984.

(Harold Appleyard)

The British Waterways Board was responsible for most towage on the major canals in the British Isles. The Gloucester and Sharpness Canal was home to a number of smaller tugs including the **Severn Iris** seen here on 16 September 1963. She is just south of Gloucester with a bucket dredger and spoil barge in tow.. Most of these tugs had been built with steam propulsion but were later converted to motor. The **Severn Iris** was built as the **Iris**, but records do not indicate when or by whom. She passed to the Admiralty at some stage, but by 1923 had been put to work with the Sharpness New Docks and Gloucester and Birmingham Canal. Upon passing to the newly formed British Waterways Board, she lost her steam plant in 1954 gaining a 4-cylinder Ruston & Hornsby engine of 240bhp. At some stage in the early 1960s she became the **Severn Iris** and was sold in the 1970s losing her R&H diesel. Still in the Bristol Channel area she was re-engined for use as a leisure craft shortly after and continued as such until 1997 when she sailed for Barrow-in-Furness. As of 2002 she was laid up in the Duddon Estuary.

(John Wiltshire)

For the author, this is what memories are made of. The steam tug **Dunhawk** and motor tug **Duncurlew** have just brought an ore carrier into the lock at Newport. As the stern tugs, they have just cast off and will hand over to the dock tugs of the British Transport Docks Board, which will berth the ship. The **Dunhawk** was built as the **Empire Maisie** in 1943. Delivered from Henry Scarr's yard at Hessle, she had a triple expansion engine of 1000ihp. A member of the Birch Class of Empire tug, the **Empire Maisie** became the **Flying Typhoon** of Clyde Shipping in 1947.

In September 1960, as part of its fleet modernisation programme, she was sold and purchased by the Newport Screw Towing Co. During her eight years at Newport she worked alongside two other Empire type tugs, the **Dunfalcon** and **Duneagle**. By 1966 the **Duneagle** had been sold, and the **Dunhawk** had become the preferred regular steam tug working alongside the motor tugs **Duncurlew** and **Dunsnipe**. She was withdrawn and, along with the **Dunfalcon,** sold for scrap to J Cashmore, of Newport, in 1968.

(John Wiltshire)

In 1962 Newport Screw Towing took delivery of a pair of new motor tugs in an attempt to modernise its ailing fleet. The **Duncurlew** was the first to be delivered and was built by Richard Dunston at Hessle. Her main engine was a 6-cylinder British Polar two-stroke diesel of 1260bhp. This gave her a bollard pull of 22 tonnes. Despite her power and age, she did not have bridge control of her main engine which made her unpopular in later years. Newport Screw Towing sold out to Cory Ship Towage in 1971 and four tugs were included in the deal. The **Duncurlew** eventually became the **Westgarth** and continued to serve Newport until her sale in 1981 to Norwegian owners. She sailed north to her new home port of Narvik carrying the name **Nord Beaver**. She is still sailing today although her superstructure has been much altered and she no longer has her Polar diesel. This view out in the Bristol Channel on 21 May 1971 shows off her 101 feet length to good effect. She is wearing her newly-acquired Cory colours but has yet to change her name.

(Danny Lynch)

Wyegarth was the former Newport dock tug **St. Woolas** of 1960, which was by now operating for Cory Ship Towage. She was ordered by the British Transport Commission and built by P K Harris at Appledore. Her sister was the **Llanwern**, which differed in that she had diesel-electric propulsion. Both had Lister Blackstone engines of 1200bhp. They worked principally at Newport alongside the older motor tug **Newport** until 1977, when the British Transport Docks Board sold its towage interests at Newport to Cory Ship Towage. The **Wyegarth** was not popular with crews despite being twin-screw and was not a good sea vessel. The early morning sunshine creates an atmospheric scene as she heads out from Newport on 6 April 1980. The **Wyegarth** was eventually sold in 1981, and left Newport for a new home in Saudi Arabia as the **Rana.** Registered at Jeddah, she was renamed **Zaretallah** shortly after her arrival there. She is still thought to be in service.

(Danny Lynch)

Another former Empire tug to work in south-east Wales was the **Hallgarth** of 1943. She was one of only two examples of the Modified Hornby class, and was launched as **Empire Joan**. She was built by Cochrane & Sons, of Selby, and had a gross tonnage of 203 grt. Her steam plant was by McKie and Baxter and produced 800ihp. In 1947 she was renamed **Emphatic** and took up duties with the Admiralty at Chatham. She was withdrawn in 1958 with stability problems and put up for sale. She passed to Cardiff tug operator E Hancock and kept her name. By 1963 she was still working at Cardiff and Barry, but in the ownership of R & J H Rea Ltd, and named **Hallgarth.** Wholesale replacement of steam tugs at Cardiff and Barry took place between 1965 and 1966, and the **Hallgarth** was sold to J Cashmore at Newport for scrap in May 1966.

(Danny Lynch collection)

This view on 9 March 1969 at Cardiff gives us an opportunity to compare three Rea motor tugs of similar size but from three different shipyards. Nearest the camera is the **Polgarth** which dates from 1962 and is visiting Cardiff from Avonmouth. She was a product of Hill's shipyard in Bristol. Alongside her is the **Plumgarth** of 1960, sister of the **Avongarth** (see page 16). She was built at the Yarwood yard in Northwich. Alongside is the **Danegarth** built by Richards of Lowestoft in 1966. The old steamship in the background is the **Maria M.** which was laid up for a while in the Queen Alexandra Dock at Cardiff. The **Polgarth** would probably return to Avonmouth on the next high tide after Cardiff had finished with her. It was usually the **Polgarth** or **Pengarth** that came across to Cardiff to help out when traffic was busy.

(John Wiltshire)

The **Lowgarth**, seen on page 20, was the forerunner of four similar tugs destined for R & J H Rea at Cardiff and Barry in 1966. They were ordered rather hastily and would replace the last of the steam tugs. The third to be delivered was the **Danegarth** built by Richards Shipbuilders. She was launched at Lowestoft on 7 February 1966 and is seen here on 29 March 1975 in the colours of Cory Ship Towage. Unlike the **Lowgarth**, the **Danegarth** and her three sisters had a Blackstone engine. Other minor differences were the size of the port and starboard wheelhouse windows and the use of a jib in place of lifeboat davits as

found on the **Lowgarth**. The **Danegarth** remained at Cardiff until 1979 when she was displaced by the arrival of two new tractor tugs. She was transferred to Newport, changing her colours in 1985 when her owner was restyled Cory Towage Ltd. In 1992 the **Danegarth** was sold to Greek owners Pangolas Compania and became the **Linoperamata.** She changed hands in 1993 passing to Linoperamata Shipping who put her to work based at the Crete port of Heraklion. She is still in service in 2006.

(John Wiltshire)

Until 1983 Cory's Newport based tug fleet really did seem to be a bit of refuge for the company's older or obscure vessels. The **Cultra** was a one such tug, and arrived from the Belfast fleet in 1980. She was delivered to James Cooper, of Belfast, in 1962 as their second new motor tug based at the port. She was built by Mitchison, of Gateshead. The **Cultra** was completed on 2 August 1962 with a Swedish-built Polar diesel of 1260bhp. She had a hydroconic hull, and featured twin exhaust uptakes and a walkway around the front of her wheelhouse. The business of J Cooper passed to R & J H Rea in 1969, which in turn passed to Cory

Ship Towage Ltd in 1970. The arrival at Newport in 1983 of a modern compact former German motor tug saw the **Cultra** put up for sale. She passed to Frank Pearce, of Poole, by whom she was renamed **Pulwell**. In 1985 she headed for Greece and became the **Polikos** in the fleet of Boukos Tugs. She was still sailing in 2006 for Portolos Salvage at Piraeus. The **Cultra** is seen here working at Cardiff on 25 July 1982. By 2006 the background had been obscured by the Cardiff Bay Barrage.

(Andrew Wiltshire)

When completed in 1911 the **Bristolian** was the most powerful tug at Bristol and reputed to be the fastest tug in the Bristol Channel. She was bought to cope with the increasing size of liners calling at Avonmouth at the time. The **Bristolian** was constructed at Leith by J Cran and was 174 gross tons. She had a compound expansion steam engine and was originally certified to carry 199 passengers. By the 1960s this very elegant looking vessel had become the reserve tug in King's Avonmouth fleet, and remained coal-fired. Her appearance had changed little over the years. The **Bristolian**'s days were numbered in this view as we see her sailing from Barry. The reason for her visit to Barry was purely for coaling. In fact if you study her aft deck there are traces of coal that didn't quite make her bunkers. The **Bristolian** was broken up by J Cashmore at Newport in 1968, aged 57 years.

(Bob Allen)

In the author's opinion, the **Westgarth** was the ultimate in British steam tug design. She was completed for R & J H Rea Ltd. in 1954 by Charles Hill, of Bristol, for service at Avonmouth docks. Although by no means the last steam powered tug to be built for service in the UK, her lines were clean and more akin to that of a motor tug. The drawing office at Charles Hill was always ahead of the times. She had a modern-looking wheelhouse and her funnel, although tall, was unusually slender. When Rea set up its operation at Cardiff and Barry in October 1961, she moved across to be based at Cardiff. She is seen here at Barry in 1966 assisting

a tanker into the lock with the **Lowgarth** as the bow tug. The **Westgarth** was sold to Italian buyers later that year having been replaced by more modern motor tugs. She would have been a good buy at 12 years of age. Renamed **Serapo** she served with Rimorchiatori Napoletani at the ports of Naples and Bari in southern Italy. She was their last steam tug. Tragically she was rammed and sunk by a ferry at Bari in August 1990. This was a very sad end to a survivor and a good-looking tug.

(Bob Allen)

Here we see another tug that has been sent across from Avonmouth to help out, at Barry this time. The date was 6 August 1969, and the **Falgarth** can be seen assisting with the docking of a tanker. Launched in the Netherlands on 3 July 1958 as the **Cleddia**, she was the second of a pair of tugs ordered by the Overseas Towage and Salvage Co for use at Milford Haven. Along with her sister **Neylandia**, she passed to R & J H Rea Ltd in 1961 for use at Avonmouth and Bristol and was renamed **Falgarth**. She remained based at this port passing to Cory Ship Towage in 1970. In 1972 she was transferred to the new Cory unit at Plymouth set up following the acquisition of the Reynolds towage business. She was eventually sold to Delos Maritime of Piraeus in 1980 as the **Aetos**. After disappearing from *Lloyds Register*, and a period of uncertainty, she was discovered still in service in 2004. In very good condition, she was based on the Greek island of Milos, and bore the appropriate name **Milos**.

(Nigel Jones)

A choppy sea, sunshine and a gathering of storm clouds. Dramatic conditions just off Swansea's breakwaters on 20 November 1970 as the steam tug **Canning** proceeds out into Swansea Bay with her tow. The sun catches the beach, but things look distinctly gloomy over the rest of Swansea. The **Canning** was the last of a trio of steam tugs built in 1954 by Cochrane & Sons, of Selby, for Alexandra Towing Co, of Liverpool. She remained based at Liverpool until transferred to Swansea in 1966. She was notably the last steam tug to operate in the Bristol Channel when she finally retired in 1975. The **Canning** then passed to the local Industrial and Maritime Museum in Swansea for preservation. In 2006 she was drydocked and smartened up, and can now be found moored adjacent to the National Waterfront Museum in Swansea.

(John Wiltshire)

The **Wapping** was a temporary addition to the Alexandra Towing fleet at Swansea. We see her hard at work in the Kings Dock on the sunny morning of 29 September 1972. She was new in 1959 as the first motor tug delivered to the Liverpool fleet of J H Lamey Ltd. As the **William Lamey** she was built on the banks of the River Tyne by Mitchison, of Gateshead. She was not launched in the conventional manner, but lifted into the water by a floating crane. She had two Lister Blackstone engines geared to a single shaft and her hull was to the then popular hydroconic design. She became the **Wapping** in 1970 after J H Lamey was taken over by Alexandra Towing Co. From Swansea she moved to the Gibraltar fleet in 1973 where she stayed until 1975, before returning to the Mersey. She was sold to Greek interests in 1985 and became the **Theodoros 1** of Atlantic Tugs Maritime. In 2002 she passed to Star Bunkering of Piraeus as the **Agios Rafail**. She was under the Liberian flag as the **Fox 1** a year later and remains in service in 2006 but now flying the flag of Honduras.

(John Wiltshire)

This view really does seem to illustrate two classic tugs, one steam and the other motor, working together in harmony. At the entrance to the Queens Dock at Swansea, the **North Buoy** and **Alexandra** are hard at work on the stern of a tanker. The **North Buoy** is an identical sister to the **North Wall** both built in 1959 and the last steam tugs delivered to a UK fleet. The **Alexandra** by contrast was built in 1963, and was a product of Yarwood's Northwich yard. She was a sister tug to the **Herculaneum** of 1962. The **Alexandra** arrived at Swansea in 1966 from

Liverpool, whereas the **North Buoy** migrated from the Mersey in 1969. The date is 2 July 1971 and there were still five steam tugs working at Swansea and Port Talbot. The **North Buoy** had two years left at Swansea whereas the **Alexandra** went on to give another 27 years service at the port before being sold in 1998. She passed to GPS Marine Contractors Rochester Ltd, and can still be seen around the British Isles employed on coastal towing work.

(John Wiltshire)

The construction of a new large tidal harbour at Port Talbot to handle large bulk carriers brought with it new challenges for the Alexandra Towing Co. To service this new facility they ordered two large motor tugs from Richard Dunston's yard at Hessle near Hull. The first of these, the **Mumbles**, was delivered on 16 February 1969 to Port Talbot. A very impressive looking tug with a high fo'c'sle and large wheelhouse, she was powered by a 9-cylinder Ruston Diesel of 2190 bhp driving a single propeller in a Kort Nozzle. The **Mumbles** boasted a bollard pull of 40 tonnes and was fitted with a salvage pump. Based at Swansea she was often used on coastal towing and when new actually towed some of the steam tugs she

replaced to the breakers near Cork. She is seen here at Swansea moving towards the lock entrance on 10 October 1969 with a ship in tow. She was followed in 1970 by the similar but slightly lower profile **Margam.** Alexandra Towing was taken over by the Howard Smith group in 1992 and the colour scheme changed. Later the **Mumbles** was transferred to its Gibraltar operation. Since 1998 she has been working for TP Towage, the local tug fleet at Gibraltar, and still carrying her original name. Back in Swansea, Howard Smith closed its Swansea office in late 1998 and pulled out of the port altogether.

(John Wiltshire)

As the size of tankers continued to grow in the 1970s, so the need for larger and more powerful tugs became apparent. The **Eyegarth** was the final member of a quartet of 3520bhp single-screw estuary tugs for Milford Haven. The order was originally split equally between Richards Shipbuilders and the Drypool Group at Beverley. Drypool was in financial difficulties and only managed to complete the **Exegarth** in 1976. Work had just started on the **Eyegarth** and this was subsequently transferred to Richards at Great Yarmouth. Delivered in April 1977 she had a 16-cylinder Ruston diesel engine and an impressive bollard pull of 50 tonnes. Like the **Exegarth** she was fitted for firefighting. On 18 June 1991 we see the **Eyegarth** heading down the Haven past the disused Esso jetty in bright but unsettled weather conditions. Of note is the Cory title in large letters on the superstructure. The tug fleet at Milford Haven was scaled down in 1995, and the **Eyegarth** was sold to Far Eastern buyers together with the **Exegarth**. The pair was noted in the Philippines in 1999, by which time the **Eyegarth** carried the name **Pagbilao 11.** She is thought to be still in service as she appears in the 2006/7 edition of *Lloyd's Register*.

(Andrew Wiltshire)

The **Weather Cock** was built in 1960 for North West Tugs, a subsidiary of Liverpool Screw Towing known locally as "Cock Tugs". She was the final vessel in a series of five motor tugs delivered in the late 1950s to modernise the elderly post-war fleet. All were built locally by Cammell Laird at Birkenhead. The **Weather Cock** was to the later improved style with a very box-like wheelhouse and had a 1060 bhp Ruston & Hornsby engine. The **Weather Cock,** however, unlike her sisters had the bonus of a two-speed gearbox. In 1968 the Liverpool Screw Towing operations passed to the Alexandra Towing Company and the **Weather Cock** became the **Formby** in 1970. In 1981 all the former Liverpool Screw Towing motor tugs were sold to Vernicos Shipping of Piraeus. They were despatched in two separate groups. The **Formby** became the **Vernicos Alexia** and was one of three tugs wrecked on the Pembrokeshire coast near Solva on 18 October 1981. The other two were the former **Heath Cock** and **Pea Cock**. In happier times we see her off Birkenhead on 23 August 1970.

(Paul Boot)

On the same day we see the **Alfred Lamey** too. The old established Liverpool tug business of J H Lamey Ltd eventually sold its operations to Alexandra Towing in July 1968. Included in the deal were seven motor tugs. The **Alfred Lamey** was new in 1967 and followed the design first introduced in 1959 by the **William Lamey** (see page 31). The **Alfred Lamey** was completed on the Clyde by James Lamont and had a German MWM diesel of 1776bhp. The Lamey company was noted for its innovations in tug operation on the Mersey. For example they were the first fleet to use motor tugs, VHF radio and radar. The **Alfred Lamey** went on to acquire the name **Coburg** in the Alexandra Towing fleet and was transferred to Southampton for a period in the mid-1970s. Eventually after returning to the Mersey she was sold in 1993 to Norwegian tug owner Peder Arnesen as the **Mor**. She later became the **Argus** in 1998 and was sailing in 2006 as the **Khan** still under the Norwegian flag.

(Paul Boot)

The Rea Towing Co Ltd, of Liverpool, had a class of six elegant-looking steam tugs delivered in the early 1950s. They were all built by Alexander Hall, of Aberdeen, and were coal fired. Their lines closely followed those of tugs built for Rea Towing in the 1920s but were larger vessels and more powerful. A feature of Rea Towing tugs for many years was the enclosed side passage. The *Grassgarth* was delivered in 1953 and her boiler was converted to burn oil in 1959. Her triple expansion engine had an output of 1120ihp. Rea Towing tugs were normally named after trees, the *Grassgarth* being an exception to this rule. She was withdrawn from service in 1970 and sold in the December to a Dublin owner together with two of her sister ships *Aysgarth* and *Throstlegarth*. In the event they were never collected from the Mersey, and in 1972 were sold to shipbreakers at Troon.

(Malcolm Donnelly)

Rea Ltd, part of the Rea Towing Company, took over the small towage business of Wm Bate & Co in 1960 and with it came a pair of elderly steam tugs. To replace these they ordered two motor tugs from W J Yarwood at Northwich which were delivered as the *Elmgarth* and *Pinegarth*. A third similar tug was later ordered and appeared as the *Cherrygarth* in 1963. The *Elmgarth* is seen here in Liverpool docks in August 1970 with T & J Harrison's *Diplomat* in the background. The *Elmgarth* was launched ten years earlier on 15 June 1960 and could best be described as a barge-towing tug. She was somewhat top-heavy in appearance and a mere 68 feet in length. The main engine was a 6-cylinder Ruston and Hornsby of 400bhp. She was sold in 1972 to Lowestoft-based Pevensey Castle Ltd who renamed her *Barkis.* On 16 August 1976 she was struck by the Cypriot-flagged *Jupiter* (1594grt/64) off Lowestoft while passing a line to her. The *Barkis* capsized and eventually sank half a mile north of the Lowestoft piers.

(Andrew Wiltshire collection)

The **Sloyne** was built as the **Fighting Cock** in 1953 for the Liverpool Screw Towing subsidiary North West Tugs. She and her sistership the **Gamecock V** were launched on 12 May 1953 at Cammell Laird's Birkenhead yard. They were modern-looking coal-fired steam tugs of 218 grt and 1250ihp. In 1960 they were converted to oil burning and both had the height of the funnels reduced drastically. Liverpool Screw Towing, as mentioned earlier, disappeared into the Alexandra Towing empire and the **Fighting Cock** eventually acquired the less glamorous but traditional Alexandra name **Sloyne**. Here we see her out on the Mersey on 20 April 1971 with the Liver Building dominating the background. The pair were sold to Vernicos Shipping of Piraeus later in 1971 and the **Sloyne** became the **Vernicos Nicos**. She was broken up in 1988.

(Paul Boot)

The smallest operator of ship-handling tugs on the Mersey in the 1960s was Johnston Warren Lines Ltd. In 1958 the company replaced its three steam tugs with three attractive motor tugs. One of these was the **Rossmore** which was built at Bristol by Charles Hill and finished to a very high standard. She was 206 grt and had a 7-cylinder Ruston & Hornsby diesel of 1200bhp. Johnston Warren sold its towage interests to Rea Towing Ltd in 1968 and the **Rossmore** became the **Rossgarth**. She makes a fine sight underway in the Eastham Channel on 16 July 1972, her last summer on the Mersey. Unlike her two sisters (by now named

Foylegarth and **Kilgarth** and which lasted into the 1980s), the **Rossgarth** was sold prematurely in 1972. She passed to the Mediterranean Ship Towage for use at Valletta in Malta. In 1981 she was renamed **Rozi** when she passed Tug Malta Ltd. She was pensioned off in 1992 and sold to local pleasure boat owner Captain Morgan Cruises. She was then sunk as an artificial reef off the coast of Malta. This was with the intention of running submarine trips to the wreck site for tourists. An unusual end indeed.

(Paul Boot)

The **Daniel Adamson** story is one of a remarkable survivor. Built as long ago as 1903, she was completed as the **Ralph Brocklebank**, a tug/tender for the Shropshire Union Canal and Railway Co. Her builder was the long-ceased Tranmere Bay Development Company, of Birkenhead. She was sometimes used for passenger-carrying duties, but principally for barge towing between Ellesmere Port and Liverpool. Together with her two sisters this continued until 1915 after which she was confined to towing only. She passed to the Manchester Ship Canal Company in 1921 and was modified in 1929, and later rebuilt with a raised wheelhouse in 1936. At this time she became the **Daniel Adamson** and resumed the role of tender tug and inspection vessel on the Manchester Ship Canal. This continued for 48 years until 1984 when she was taken out of service. She became an exhibit at the Ellesmere Port Maritime Museum soon after, but over the years gradually fell into a very poor state of repair. As the call to the breakers yard beckoned, a rescue attempt in 2004 proved successful and she was saved. The **Daniel Adamson** Preservation Society was formed and the vessel moved to a dry dock in Liverpool for inspection. Now the subject of a mammoth restoration project, she is a twin-screw vessel with a pair of compound steam engines of 500ihp combined output and built by J Jones & Sons, Liverpool. She will be a worthy working exhibit when complete. She is seen underway on the Canal near Warrington on 5 July 1972.

(Paul Boot)

The **MSC Tarn** is seen making her way along the canal on 10 October 1977. The Manchester Ship Canal Co started introducing motor tugs for ship handling on the canal in 1939. They were usually ordered in pairs. All were twin-screw and earlier examples were built by Henry Robb at Leith. The **MSC Tarn** was one of a pair delivered in 1961 by P K Harris, of Appledore. She was 124 grt and had a pair of Ruston & Hornsby engines giving a total of 1210bhp. An unusual but understandable feature of ship canal tugs was that there was no provision for an anchor. She was a functional tug with twin exhaust uptakes, her sister ship being the **MSC Talisman**. In 1981 the **MSC Tarn** was sold to Salvor 1 Shipping of Greece and named **Salvor 1.** After several changes of ownership it has been established that she still sails in 2006 as the Georgian-flagged **Triton**.

(Paul Boot)

Preston dock was situated along the River Ribble and was formally opened on 25 June 1892. During the 1950s an elderly fleet of steam tugs was gradually replaced by four compact twin screw motor tugs.

On 28 August 1968 we see the **John Herbert** towing the Russian freighter **Kohtla** towards the lock at Preston. **John Herbert** was built in 1955 by Henry Robb at Leith and had twin 5-cylinder Crossley diesels with an output of 720bhp. The stern tug which we also see in close up is the identical **Frank Jamieson** built in 1956. On this occasion she is using a single rope stern to stern. Apparently, this method had never been used before at Preston. Crossed wires over the bow were the norm. The final view shows the Norwegian **Skotfoss** of 1952 being rescued in the River Ribble by the **John Herbert** and **Hewitt** (of 1951), after suffering engine failure. The tide is falling fast and she is eventually put safely aground ready to be refloated on the next tide.

After service at Preston, the **John Herbert** went on to sail in the Middle East, being noted by the author at Basrah in 1980. She was reported to be named **Sinbad Glory** in 2006. The **Frank Jamieson** later served James Fisher at Barrow and the **Hewitt** was sold to Greek owners..

(Alick Hadwen)

The first of many Voith-Schneider tractor tugs for Alexandra Towing appeared at Liverpool in 1980/81. The **Canada** was built locally by McTay Marine at Bromborough whilst the more or less identical **Collingwood** came from the Dunston yard at Hessle. The **Collingwood** has a pair of Voith-Schneider propulsion units driven by two Ruston Diesels delivering 2640bhp. As well as working from their base at Liverpool, Alexandra would from time to time be called upon to provide towage at Heysham and Barrow-in-Furness. She is seen sailing from Heysham on a fine day, 5 May 1988. Following the 1992 takeover by Howard Smith Towage, the **Collingwood** had her funnels reduced in height to improve visibility from her wheelhouse. In 1999 Howard Smith sold its towage business to another Australian company, Adsteam.

(Paul Boot)

The **Salisbury** is another example of a TID class tug for the Ministry of War Transport. In total 182 TIDs were built between 1943 and 1946. She was an early example completed in 1943 as the **TID 15**. She finished her military service in September 1946 which included a spell with the US Army. Finally in 1949 she was bought by Bristol based lighter man Benjamin Perry and Sons and renamed **B.P.2**. In 1957 she became the **Salisbury** and in 1964 she was converted to motor at the Charles Hill shipyard where a 350bhp Ruston & Hornsby engine was fitted. She was sold in 1980 and by 1981 was working in the Isle of Man for Laxey Towing. Here we see her crossing Douglas Bay on 28 August 1982. In 1992 she passed to Hunter Marine of Greystones, County Wicklow, and became the **Delgany**. As such she was with Bere Island Ferries by 1998 and was noted in a bad state of repair at Bere Island, County Cork, in September 2002.

(Nigel Jones)

Here is another splendid example of a World War 2 Empire type tug. This time we have a member of the Hoedic Class. Completed in 1943 by Cochrane & Sons, of Selby, as *Empire Denis*, she saw wartime service in the Mediterranean at Malta and Italy. Returning to the UK she passed to Clyde Shipping in 1947 as the *Flying Meteor*. She is seen here on the upper reaches of the River Clyde near Dalmuir East on 5 May 1961. Clyde Shipping replaced her in 1962 with a motor tug and the *Flying Meteor* sailed south to a new owner in South Wales at Cardiff. In the ownership of I C Guy Ltd, she became the *Royal Rose*. This business passed to R & J H Rea on 30 June 1963 and the *Royal Rose* went on to become the *Yewgarth*. Just over two years later in September 1965 disaster struck. Whilst assisting the ore carrier *Aldersgate* into the lock at Cardiff she was struck and started to sink. The tug *Tregarth* was close at hand, took the *Yewgarth* in tow and managed to beach her. She was declared a loss and towed to Newport to be scrapped shortly after this.

(Bernard Kent)

The **Warrior** was built in 1935 by Scott & Sons, of Bowling, as a steam tug for Steel and Bennie Ltd, of Glasgow. She had a triple expansion engine of 112nhp. Her design was to be the basis for the Warrior class of Empire tug of which five examples were built in the early 1940s. After the war Steel and Bennie bought one new steam tug and a number of former Empire tugs. In the 1950s, however, they embarked upon a fleet modernisation programme. This involved the delivery of a number of new motor tugs and the conversion to motor of three steam tugs. The **Warrior** was one of those selected and received a 1200bhp Widdop diesel in 1958. The boiler was retained to maintain trim and was usually fully primed. Eleven years later in 1969 she was sold to Falmouth Towage and renamed **St. Agnes**. Despite her age she put in some good service at the Cornish port. She was retired in 1985 and broken up at Sittingbourne.

(Malcolm Donnelly)

Remarkably, the Ministry of Defence was still operating two former Empire tugs in the 1970s. The **Prompt** was based at Portsmouth and the **Eminent** on the Clyde. The **Eminent** is seen here in glorious sunshine on the Clyde, her superstructure being grey as opposed to the more common buff. Of note is the heavy bow fender arrangement to assist with the handling of submarines. The **Eminent** was built in 1946 by W Simons, of Renfrew, as **Empire Tessa** and was a member of the Improved Stella class. Of 302 grt, she had an output of 800ihp at 120rpm. Eleven examples were built to meet a specific requirement for undertaking long voyages with light tows. They had a good displacement and large bunker capacity; they were also fitted with salvage and firefighting pumps. All 11 in the class had oil-fired boilers from new. They were popular with crews as they were good sea keeping vessels. They were also equipped to work in tropical climates. As **Empire Tessa**, she was initially based in Bermuda where she later changed her name to **Eminent**. She returned to the UK in 1951 with fire damage and was repaired at Portsmouth. In 1969 she moved north to the Clyde. Upon sale in 1976, she became the **Goliath** of ITL International Towing Co Ltd and was used on coastal towing occasionally, alongside the **Cervia** (page 5). She eventually passed to the Maryport Maritime Museum in 1983, but was scrapped at Millom in February 1986. She was in poor shape and surplus to the needs of the museum.

(Malcolm Donnelly)

The **Campaigner** is seen passing Esso's Dunglass oil terminal on 27 August 1976 and heading downstream. She was a unit of Cory Ship Towage's Clyde-based fleet and was built in 1957 for Steel and Bennie Ltd. Her sistership was the **Wrestler**. She was built at Port Glasgow by James Lamont and has an uncommon 8-cylinder Widdop diesel of 1065bhp. At 248 grt she is a large vessel for her power. She was pensioned off in 1977 and snapped up by Frank Pearce (Tugs), of Poole who named her **Pullwell Victor**. She was put to work on coastal towing. This lasted until 1981 when she sailed for a new life in Greece as the **Marambu**. She subsequently became the **Kappa** of Kappa Maritime, Piraeus, and was noted derelict at Perama by 2004. Shortly after this she was towed to Turkey and broken up at Aliaga.

(Nigel Jones)

Clyde Shipping bought three smaller motor tugs in 1959/60. One, the **Flying Dolphin**, was of German build, but the **Flying Wizard** and her sister **Flying Witch** came from the yard of J L Thompson & Sons at Sunderland in 1960. This yard was usually associated with the construction of larger ships. The tugs were powered by a 1060bhp Deutz oil engine and were 116 grt. She is seen leaving Greenock. The deep orange band on her hull was for years a trademark of Clyde Shipping. Sadly the **Flying Wizard** sank in an incident at Greenock in 1971 and after salvage was sold to H Pounds, of Portsmouth, for renovation and resale. She was renamed **Towing Wizard** by Pounds in 1975. Having been sold on, she was sailing in Greek waters as the **Alexandros** by 1978 for Gigilinis of Thessaloniki. She sank for the second time in her career in November 2002, whilst towing.

(Malcolm Donnelly)

Aberdeen has always been a busy port, initially with the fishing industry and since the 1960s has been associated with the offshore oil industry. There have never been many tugs kept at the port though. The Aberdeen Steam Tug Company had 4 steam tugs: **Danny**, **Glen**, **Ness** and **Ridgway**. In 1962 things changed when the Harbour Board placed in service a pair of modern motor tugs. They were named **Sea Griffon** and **Sea Trojan** and both were built locally by J Lewis. Of very plain appearance, they were single-screw tugs with an engine built by the National Gas and Oil Engine Company, a very rare installation in a tug. The **Sea Griffon** had a bollard pull of 14.5 tonnes and was to serve at Aberdeen for 32 years. She is seen here underway in April 1975 with a couple of supply vessels moored nearby. She was sold in 1994 to Fife Marine at Kinross and by 1999 had passed to Coastal Marine of Peterhead. Although still in existence in 2006, the **Sea Griffon** has been laid up at Dundee out of use since about 2002.

(Andrew Wiltshire collection)

The port of Grangemouth was opened in 1843 and is located on the southern shore of the Firth of Forth upstream from the famous Forth Bridges. By the 1970s Grangemouth was handling containers as well as oil and car imports. The local tug company Grangemouth and Forth Towing operated a fleet of around five tugs at any one time. The **Dalgrain** of 1963 and 129 grt was a follow-on from the earlier **Zetland** of 1961. Both were built locally by the Grangemouth Dockyard Co Ltd. She is seen here having just picked up her tow, a Hamburg America Line freighter, and will commence the approach to the lock. The date is October 1969 and Kincardine Power Station can just be discerned in the background. Her lines are quite unusual and Scandinavian in appearance, whilst her power unit is of Danish origin, being a 7-cylinder B&W built under licence by Alpha Diesel. Both the **Zetland** and **Dalgrain** were replaced at Grangemouth in 1979 by the modern tractor tugs **Laggan** and **Carron**. Like so many British tugs the **Dalgrain** found further service in Greece as the **Sekavin 2** of Piraeus-based Sekavin S.A.

(Andrew Wiltshire collection)

In 1972 Grangemouth and Forth Towing sold out, with Cory Ship Towage and the Clyde Shipping Company each taking a 50% share of the business. A few years later the new company was awarded the contract for towage at the Hound Point oil terminal further downstream near Leith. This required four new much larger purpose-built tugs. Grangemouth and Forth Towing was restyled Forth Tugs Ltd in 1977. The **Forth** of 1968 is seen in the Grangemouth dock system in June 1977. She was built by Scott & Sons, of Bowling, and is 184 grt. The **Forth** was the third new motor tug for the fleet and had very distinctive lines. She was sold in 1984 to the Port Authority at Dundee and became the **Abertay**. She still operates to this day, but is restricted to the confines of the Dundee docks.

(Andrew Wiltshire collection)

When the **Gunnet** was new in 1967, Voith-Schneider tractor tugs were still very much unheard of in most British tug fleets. The Leith Dock Commissioners took a pair in 1967 to replace, by complete contrast, two elderly steam tugs. The second vessel was named **Inchcolm**; both were local names. They were compact and rather stylish tugs and were built by J Lewis of Aberdeen, not usually associated with tug construction. They had twin Voith units and a bollard pull of 15 tonnes. In 1970 ownership passed to the Forth Ports Authority and a third more powerful tractor was delivered in 1978 named **Oxcar**, followed by another even larger pair in 1983. After a spell as a reserve tug the **Gunnet** was sold in 1990 to Klyne Tugs, of Lowestoft, and renamed **Anglianman**. She was based for a period at Ramsgate. She then passed to Cory Towage in 1995 specifically for use at Hartlepool and was renamed **Ingleby Cross** in 1996. She was not popular with crews, and after a brief move to the Tyne fleet, was sold in 1998 to Bilberry Shipping at Waterford. In 2004 she passed to the Gibraltar subsidiary Sunwood Shipping. The **Gunnet** is seen here when quite new on 11 May 1968, underway in Leith docks. In the background is part of the shipyard of Henry Robb Ltd.

(Bernard Kent)

The port of Blyth was for many years a major coal exporting port. It was also home to shipbuilding and repair yards as well as a substantial shipbreaking yard. The Blyth Tug Company kept a number of tugs at Blyth in the late 1950s and early 1960s, one of which was the elderly **Langton** of 1892. She was built for the Alexandra Towing Co, Liverpool, by S McKnight & Co Ltd, Ayr, and had a 580ihp compound steam engine built by Muir & Houston, of Glasgow. She moved to the Tyne in 1909 under the ownership of J Batey. Capable of 10 knots, she was this

owner's first screw-driven tug. She was requisitioned for war service from 1915 to 1920 before passing back to Lawson Batey Tugs. The **Langton** passed to the associated Blyth Tug Company fleet in 1953. Here we see her entering the port past the East Pier on 7 April 1962. Her days were nearly over as she was laid up later that year and broken up at Gateshead by J J King in May 1963. The **Langton** was a coal-fired tug.

(Bernard Kent)

52

The **Francis Batey** was built in 1914 by Hepple & Co at South Shields. She was built for J Batey of Newcastle who specified a compound steam engine with an output of 750ihp and speed of 12 knots. The tug saw Admiralty service in both wars, returning to service with Lawson Batey tugs in 1942. Whilst towing a tanker on the Tyne in December 1946 she sank; thankfully all her crew were saved. The **Francis Batey** was raised and put back into service within 6 months. She is seen here in August 1961 assisting the passenger ship **Parkeston** of 1925 on to No.11 berth on Newcastle Corporation Quayside. She is in the colours of Tyne Tugs Ltd. This was a consortium set up in 1959 by Lawson Batey Tugs, France, Fenwick (Tyne & Wear) and Ridley Tugs Ltd to operate tugs on charter on the River Tyne. The **Francis Batey** moved to the Blyth Tug Co fleet in 1962 to replace the **Langton** (see page 52). She became a reserve tug and saw little use, and was finally broken up at the port in 1968.

(Malcolm Donnelly)

The **Cullercoats** was named after a village to the north of the River Tyne. Built as long ago as 1898 as the **Cyclop**, she was acquired in 1926 from Bureau Wijsmuller of the Netherlands. She was, however, built locally at J P Rennoldson's yard at South Shields. She was purchased by France, Fenwick Tyne & Wear Ltd and put to work on the Tyne. The **Cullercoats** was to receive a replacement triple expansion steam engine and boiler in 1956 sourced from a 1946-built French trawler. This was built by Caledon SB & E Co Ltd, Dundee, and, with an output of 700ihp, was more powerful than her original plant. In 1959 she became part of the Tyne Tugs fleet, hence her livery. At the age of 70 she succumbed to the breaker being dismantled at Dunston-on-Tyne in May 1968. Not bad service at all.

(Malcolm Donnelly)

Another steam tug seen on the Tyne is the *Wearmouth* of 1929. By pooling the resources of the three existing towage fleets, it was hoped that efficiency of towage on the Tyne would improve. Tyne Tugs did not own any tugs, but merely chartered them. The *Wearmouth* was built for France, Fenwick, Tyne & Wear Co Ltd and registered at Sunderland. She was built by Cochrane & Sons, of Selby, and had a 900ihp compound engine by Earle's Shipbuilding & Engineering Co Ltd, of Hull. The *Wearmouth* was transferred to the Tyne in 1937 and in 1959 she went on charter to Tyne Tugs. She is seen here near Tyne Dock on 17 July 1962, with Redheads shipyard and a Stag Line vessel in the background. Upon returning to Sunderland off charter in December 1966 she was the last steam tug at the port. The *Wearmouth* was broken up at Dunston-on-Tyne in January 1969.

(Bernard Kent)

Many of the steam tugs on the Tyne in the 1950s were quite elderly and replacement by modern motor tugs was seen as a priority by 1960. The **Appelsider** was one such motor tug. She was launched on 4 April 1962 and delivered to Lawson Batey Tugs, of Newcastle, in July 1962. She was ordered from the Dunston shipyard at Hessle which submitted the favoured tender based on delivery times. The exact meaning of her name is a bit of a mystery with several theories being put forward at the time. The similar tug **Westsider** appeared in 1964. The **Appelsider** had a fixed pitch propeller in a Kort Nozzle driven by a Deutz diesel engine of 1000bhp. She is seen here on 4 August 1962 when less than a month old. For some reason she was sold after only 10 years service to the Dublin Port and Docks Board and renamed the **Coliemore**. She was laid up in 2001 and by 2003 had been sold for a second time to Barcazas Dominica of the Dominican Republic. She was, however, never delivered and was lying abandoned at the Cobh Shipyard near Cork in 2005.

(Bernard Kent)

Lawson Batey Tugs ordered a pair of attractive but very basic tugs for delivery in 1980/81. They emerged from builder Richard Dunston as the **Wearsider** in November 1980 and **Tynesider** in March 1981. Not long after entering service the **Tynesider** is seen underway at speed on 26 May 1981, passing North Shields and heading up river. Upon delivery she entered service with Tyne Tugs as seen here. In 1986 Tyne Tugs was disbanded, and the fleet became known as Tyne and Wear Tugs Ltd. The colour scheme changed to the traditional buff funnel with a blue Maltese cross. The **Tynesider's** propulsion consisted of an 8-cylinder Mirrlees Blackstone engine driving a single screw in a Kort Nozzle. Output was 1125bhp and bollard pull 17 tonnes. With the dramatic downturn in traffic on the Tyne, the **Tynesider** became surplus and in the early 1990s she was sent away on charter to Glenlight Shipping. Based in Scotland, she was used to tow log carrying barges from the west coast and islands to the mainland. It was during one of these tows that she ran aground on Skate Island and sank in Loch Fyne. She was later raised and broken up at Troon in 1994 after only 13 years service.

(Michael Green)

The new colour scheme is seen here to superb effect on the tugs **Ironsider** and **Seasider**. They are working as bow tugs together in the mouth of the River Tyne on 10 June 1989. The **Ironsider** was completed in June 1967 for Lawson Batey and chartered to Tyne Tugs. She and her sister **Northsider** were 1420bhp and a more powerful version of the **Westsider** of 1964. The **Ironsider** was sold to the Greeks in 1992 as the **Megalochari XII**. The **Seasider** was completed in 1985 by Richard Dunston and was the last new tug ordered for service on the Tyne. It is appropriate that she took a traditional name. She had a controllable pitch propeller and Kort Nozzle arrangement, and this gave her a bollard pull of 18 tonnes. She joined the Cory Towage fleet in 1995 when Clyde Shipping sold its interest in Tyne and Wear Tugs Ltd. Four years later she joined the similar **Wearsider** and identical **Holmsider** in the Greek-based fleet of Karapiperis Towage. She became the **Karapiperis 16**.

(Harry Cutter)

In 1987 Humber Tugs took delivery of the first of four compact conventional tugs for use at Hull. They were of conventional propulsion, which by 1987 had become more or less obsolete for ship-handling tugs in the United Kingdom. Each had two fixed pitch propellers in Kort Nozzles. All four were completed by Cochrane Shipbuilders at Selby and had a bollard pull of around 30 tonnes. They were to have relatively short lives on the Humber and the **Lady Theresa** was sold to Clyde Shipping in 1994. She was put to work with Tyne and Wear Tugs and became the

Hillsider based on the Tyne. She is seen well underway on the Tyne on 19 July 1995. It was in this year that control of Clyde Shipping passed to Cory Towage Ltd, and in whose colours the **Hillsider** soon appeared, but without a change of name. She just survived the Wijsmuller takeover of 2001 and gained their funnel colours. Shortly after this the **Hillsider** passed to German tug owner Fairplay, of Hamburg. She became the **Fairplay XI** and was put to use at Rotterdam.

(Michael Green)

The United States Army had a standard wartime tug too, the DPC class. Unlike the Empire tugs it was motor powered and at the end of the Second World War a large number were surplus to requirements. After careful consideration France, Fenwick purchased a pair in 1950. They became the **Grangetown** and **Ryhope** and they had their deckhouse shortened and towing hook moved forward before entering service. Six months later a third example was added which became the **Cornhill**, named after a district in Sunderland like the previous two tugs. She was previously the **ST767** built in 1943 at Buffalo, New York. In 1951 motor tugs were still quite rare and this was seen as a significant step forward. All three proved to be extremely popular and reliable and after ten years a fourth example was added. The **Cornhill** had an 8-cylinder General Motors engine of 700bhp. After 29 years service on the Wear she was sold in 1980 to W G S Crouch, of Greenhithe, and named **Hannah Spearing**. Five years later she was resold and went on to have a number of further UK owners. She was eventually scrapped at Fleetwood in 1996. Here we see her on 6 July 1978 with the shipyard of Joseph L Thompson in the background.

(Michael Green)

The **Pallion** was another TID type tug and is seen here in Sunderland's South Docks whilst still steam powered. The sunshine is highlighting the fact that the bulwark plating is set in slightly thus emphasising the bracket connections. She was built as **TID 72** in 1944 and passed to the River Wear Commissioners in 1947 as the **Evelyn**. She was named **Pallion** the following year after another district in Sunderland. Along with a sister tug **Biddick** (ex **TID 54**) she continued to work on the River Wear until she was taken aside to be re-engined. She lost her tall stack and emerged as a rather characterless motor tug in 1972. When built, TIDs had an open wheelhouse and a hinged funnel. Their hull was fabricated off site in eight sections and taken by road to the shipyard. In 2006 the **Pallion** could still be found lying at Sunderland, but alas out of use.

(Harold Appleyard)

Delivered new to Sunderland in 1964, the **Dunelm** was a compact single-screw motor tug from Richard Dunston's yard. She was completed for France, Fenwick Tyne & Wear Co Ltd and had a bollard pull of 14 tonnes. In addition she had a passenger certificate for 12 persons. France, Fenwick had a very distinctive funnel colour featuring vertical blue stripes and a black anchor. Behind the tug can be seen evidence of the coal exporting facilities at Sunderland, the coal originating from the northern part of the Durham coalfield. The **Dunelm** spent her entire life in the north-east based at Sunderland until her sale in 1988. She moved down to Cornwall having been purchased by the Fowey Harbour Commissioners. This is where she can still be found in 2007, smartly turned out as the **Pendennick**.

(Michael Green)

59

The **Conservator** was certainly a classic British steam tug. She was built for use at King's Lynn in 1925. Delivered to The King's Lynn Conservancy Board from Cochrane's yard in Selby, she had a triple expansion engine built by Plenty & Son, of Newbury, which had an output of 387ihp. She remained a coal-fired tug all her life. In 1962 she was replaced by a motor tug and sold to the Seaham Harbour Dock Company. Seaham was a small but busy coal loading port just down the coast from Sunderland. Here she joined two elderly paddle tugs, the **Eppleton Hall** and **Reliant**. She is seen inbound passing the breakwaters to Seaham harbour in October 1964. Her useful life over, the **Conservator** was sold in April 1972 for breaking up at Dunston-on-Tyne.

(Bernard Kent)

In 1948 the tug fleets at ports operated by railway companies were nationalised and became the responsibility of the British Transport Commission. At Hartlepool the BTC was faced with a fleet of five ailing steam tugs that dated back to the days of the North Eastern Railway. Four new twin-screw motor tugs of 1200bhp were ordered from P K Harris, of Appledore, to replace them in 1958. They would have hydroconic hulls, large spacious wheelhouses, twin exhaust uptakes and also be fitted for firefighting. They were given local names **Hart**, **Seaton**, **Stranton** and **Throston**. The **Throston** was sold in 1961 to the Karachi Port Trust as surplus to requirements. The BTC was restyled the British Transport Docks Board in 1963 and the Hartlepool fleet passed to the newly formed Tees and Hartlepool Port Authority in 1967. The **Hart** is seen here at Hartlepool on 5 August 1981, when traffic at the port barely justified two tugs. The **Hart** became the **Port Lairge 11** in 1996 after she was sold to Bilberry Shipping, of Waterford. By 2005 she had passed to Dragatudo at Vila Franca de Xira in Portugal, and was still working in 2006.

(Michael Green)

The **Waterloo** was the second of a pair of rather top heavy looking tugs purchased by Alexandra Towing for harbour and coastal towing duties. The **Waterloo** and the **Wellington** were built in 1977 and 1976 respectively by Richard Dunston Ltd. They were in effect based on an earlier design from 1972, but with an extra deck inserted below the wheelhouse. This gave them a gross tonnage of 315. However, mechanically they were rather different from the four tugs delivered to Liverpool in 1972. They had a pair of Ruston engines of 3500bhp combined, geared to a single shaft with a controllable pitch propeller. This gave them a bollard pull of 54 tonnes. They were also fitted for firefighting. After a life of less than seven years with Alexandra Towing, the pair were sold to the Government of Iran for use at oil terminals. The **Waterloo** became the **Gorban** and was later badly damaged in the hostilities between Iran and Iraq in February 1986. It is not known if she survived this setback.

(Harold Appleyard)

Replacement of the remaining steam tugs was a priority for Tees Towing in the post-war years. The 1960-built *Erimus Cross* of 192 grt was more or less identical to the earlier *Fiery Cross* of 1957. She was built by Scott & Sons, of Bowling. Her firefighting capability made her a useful asset on the Tees with the close proximity of oil refineries and associated tank farms and terminals. Along with the *Fiery Cross* she was occasionally used for coastal towing. In 1976 she was sold to Howard Doris Ltd, of Chatham, who renamed her *Mairi of Kishorn* and employed her on contract work. She was later renamed *Carron Highlander* and was often to be found based at Kyle of Lochalsh. As such she was sold in 1999 to F H Anjary, of London, and still sails under the Panamanian flag. We see the *Erimus Cross* awaiting a launch from the Haverton Hill shipyard in the early 1970s. Behind the tug is a man-made mountain of furnace slag from the old steelworks.

(Harry Cutter)

In 1974 Tees Towing took delivery of their last tug with conventional propulsion. She was built by Richards Shipbuilders at Great Yarmouth and was suitable for coastal towing as well. Christened *Ralph Cross* she was 244 grt and 106 feet in length. She also introduced a change of main engine into the fleet. In place of the usual Crossley was a 12-cylinder Ruston of 2640bhp driving a single screw in a Kort Nozzle. The main distinguishing feature externally was her futuristic styled superstructure and wheelhouse which gave excellent all round vision. We see her on 20 April 1987 making her way up the Tees past South Bank. The *Ralph Cross* was sold to Tug Malta in 1989 and renamed *Grez*. She is still in service at Valletta in 2006.

(Harry Cutter)

Tees Towing had experimented with directional propulsion as long ago as 1958 when it bought a pair of single unit Voith-Schneider tractor tugs. These were the **Banbury Cross** and **Hutton Cross**. Eighteen years later in 1976 the **Greatham Cross** and **Skelton Cross** were delivered, and each featured a pair of Schottel rudder propellers. These were the first Schottels to be used on harbour tugs in the UK. They also incorporated the new style of superstructure and wheelhouse as originally introduced on the **Ralph Cross**. A third similar but more powerful tug, the

Yarm Cross, was delivered in 1979. She had a bollard pull of 35 tonnes provided by a pair of 6-cylinder Ruston diesels and a gross tonnage of 185. The **Yarm Cross** is seen here on 9 April 1983 having departed Tees Dock, and is heading up the Tees with the Monsanto Chemical plant in the background. Tees Towing sold out to Cory Towage in 1990 and in January 2000 the **Yarm Cross** was transferred to the Tyne fleet.

(Roy Cressey)

United Towing was the once principal tug operator at the port of Hull. It was formed in 1920 by the amalgamation of a number of smaller towage firms. In the post-war years the company continued to maintain a large fleet of mainly steam tugs. Quite a few steam tugs were built in the 1920s such as the **Headman** of 1924. She was 96 feet in length and had a triple expansion steam engine with an output of 800ihp. The **Headman** was a product of Cochrane's shipyard at Selby. Her appearance changed little in her 38 years on the Humber and for a tug operating on the east coast of England, her open wheelhouse must have been rather bracing during the winter months. She was sold in 1962, rather surprisingly, for further service. Her new owner the Blyth Tug Company renamed her **Hillsider** and got a further ten years use from her. She was finally scrapped in 1972 by Hughes Bolckow at Blyth. Here the **Headman** is approaching the lock entrance to the King George Dock, Hull on 3 April 1961.

(Bernard Kent)

The **Yorkshireman** dated from 1928 and was an altogether different tug to the **Headman**. At 251 grt she was completed by the Earle's Shipbuilding and Engineering Co, of Hull. She was twin-screw with a pair of triple-expansion units of 400ihp each. The **Yorkshireman** was built not only as a tug, but as a passenger excursion vessel. She replaced a paddle tug named **Frenchman**. For this role she had a shallow draught of less than 9 feet and was flat bottomed. One of her main duties was running trips out of Bridlington which were very popular both before and after the war. The **Yorkshireman** boasted a passenger saloon with musicians at times, and even had a small bar. Requisitioned during the war she eventually returned to Bridlington in 1951. We see her here in the King George Dock, Hull, on 3 April 1961. By the mid-1960s, being steam reciprocating and with the rising cost of coal, the **Yorkshireman** was considered uneconomical and she went to a Belgian scrapyard in 1965.

(Bernard Kent)

United Towing chose to re-engine a small number of their steam tugs in the early 1960s. The **Scotsman** of 1929 was one such vessel. A single-screw tug built by Cochrane at Selby, she started life with a 825ihp triple expansion steam engine built by Earle's Shipbuilding and Engineering Co. She was built with an open wheelhouse and two masts. In 1964 the decision was taken to fit a ten-year old 12-cylinder Mirrlees, Bickerton & Day diesel of 850bhp. She now featured a short funnel incorporating a mast which gave her an odd appearance. Her gross tonnage changed from 222 to 199 tons. Other tugs treated to diesel engines were the **Krooman**, **Norman**, **Prizeman** and the Empire tug **Serviceman**. Eight years later she was withdrawn and broken up by Albert Draper & Sons at Hull.

(Malcolm Donnelly)

Ellerman's Wilson Line was a Hull-based shipping company with a varied fleet of mainly coastal cargo ships. They had for years, however, kept a pair of tugs at Hull. The final tugs to be operated were the **Presto** of 1943 (an Empire type tug) and the slightly older **Forto** of 1939. They stood out prominently from the neighbouring United Towing vessels as they had red funnels and green hulls. The **Presto** was built by Cochrane and Son at Selby in 1943 as the **Empire Sara** and

was very similar to the **Flying Meteor** on page 45. She became the **Presto** in 1946. She is seen in splendid condition here in the lock at Hull in July 1965. Ellerman's Wilson Line sold its towing interests to United Towing in 1968 and the two tugs were laid up. Shortly after this the **Presto** was sold for scrap and broken up at Blyth by Hughes Bolckow Ltd.

(Tony and Krispen Atkinson collection)

John H Whitaker has its roots way back in 1880 when it started operating with two barges on the River Humber. Today it is a major operator of coastal and bunkering tankers throughout the British Isles. For many years the Whitaker company kept a small fleet of steam tugs at Hull for handling tank barges. One of these was the small 1920-built **Wilberforce,** 45 grt, which was very basic in appearance. She was built by the Yorkshire Drydock Company and had a Plenty & Son compound engine of 240ihp. She is seen here amongst some tank barges on 25 October 1966. The location is the St. Andrews Dock, Hull. The **Wilberforce** was broken up not long after this.

(Roy Cressey)

As well as ship handling tugs, United Towing always maintained a small fleet of barge handling tugs. These would be used around the dock system and on the River Hull. The **Riverman**, pictured underway off Hull in August 1986, started life as the River Thames tug **Brentonian** in 1955. She passed to United Towing in 1962 and became the **Bargeman** changing to **Riverman** in 1974. She was transferred to Humber Tugs at Grimsby in 1978. She was built at Appledore by P K Harris and had a 320bhp Lister Blackstone diesel. The **Riverman** was 37 grt and just over 56 feet overall length. Sold for scrap in 1995, the **Riverman** cheated the breakers and was bought by Briggs Marine Contractors shortly after and renamed **Ross End**. Sold on by 2003, she was spotted in a refurbished condition at Lowestoft in 2005.

(Harry Cutter)

United Towing purchased some fairly powerful harbour tugs in the mid-1960s for use at Hull. The **Masterman** was one of three similar vessels and was built at the Beverley shipyard of Charles D Holmes in 1964. She was a twin-screw tug of 106 feet in length. The **Masterman** had a pair of Blackstone engines with a combined output of 1320bhp and is seen in the lock at Hull on 18 June 1978. The harbour operations of United Towing became known as Humber Tugs in 1973 following the take-over of the Pigott tug fleet based at Grimsby and Immingham on the south side of the Humber. From 1984 the **Masterman** had a spell on charter to Holyhead Towing as the **Afon Wen** until 1986. She was then sold by Humber Tugs in the same year to Ektor Maritime Co of Greece and became the **Ektor**. She was still in service in Greece as the **Armos** in 2006.

(Miichael Green)

J H Pigott & Son was the principal tug operator at the port of Immingham in the 1960s. In its fleet of about nine vessels there were still a few steam tugs as late as 1966. The attractive steam tug **Lady Sarah** dated from 1909 and was built across the Humber in Hull by Earle's Shipbuilding and Engineering Co. She was 197 grt and a coal-fired boiler provided steam for her triple expansion engine. Although constructed at Hull she was to spend her first 47 years on the Thames as the **Sun 111**, in the fleet of W H J Alexander. She was one of two similar tugs, the other being the **Sun II** which was also by now in the Pigott fleet as the **Lady Thelma**. This view at Immingham dates from 24 March 1962. The **Lady Sarah** was broken up at Blyth in 1967.

(Bernard Kent)

The Pigott company took its first motor tug, the **Lady Cecilia**, in 1959. The **Lady Theresa** was a further example delivered in 1963, together with the similar **Lady Elsie**. Like the **Masterman** (page 68) she too was built inland at Beverley, but at the yard of Cook, Welton and Gemmell. She had a 7-cylinder Ruston and Hornsby engine of 920bhp. The **Lady Theresa** is seen here underway in Immingham docks on 8 September 1968. The Pigott fleet as mentioned earlier passed to Humber Tugs in 1973. A requirement for larger, more powerful tugs to work at Immingham and at the river terminals meant that the **Lady Theresa** would have a short life on the Humber. She was sold in 1974 to owners at Vancouver in Western Canada and renamed **Weldwood Spirit**. In 1994 she became the **Comox Argus** and was still sailing under the Canadian flag in 2006 as the **Yucata Spirit**.

(Roy Cressey)

J P Knight Ltd entered into a joint venture with the Orkney Islands Council to provide towage services at the new oil terminal at Flotta. For this contract Knight duly ordered two powerful twin-screw tugs from Richards of Great Yarmouth. These appeared as the **Kinloch** and **Kessock**. They were fitted with a pair of Kort Nozzles and had a bollard pull of 38 tonnes. The brand new **Kinloch** is seen here off Great Yarmouth undertaking builder's trials on 15 August 1974. In 1976 Orkney Towage was formed and the tugs changed their funnel markings to a buff colour with a local coat of arms. By 1978 they were joined at Flotta by a third larger tug the **Kintore**. In 1989 a pair of powerful stern drive tugs were delivered, and the **Kinloch** and her sister became surplus to requirements. They were modified as pusher tugs and sent to Surinam on the north-east coast of South America. Here they would be employed on one leg of a contract that Knights had obtained. This involved transporting large barges from an inland mine, downstream to a transhipment facility.

(Bob Allen)

70

Another tug seen out on builder's trials off Great Yarmouth is the **Willowgarth** of 1989. She is returning to the port on 17 July 1989. She was completed by Richards at their Great Yarmouth shipyard for Cory Towage Ltd. She was ordered for the Rea Towing Company fleet on the Mersey, and was a development of four earlier Z-Peller tugs built for them between 1981 and 1985. One duty she was intended for was tanker handling at the Tranmere oil terminal. When delivered, the **Willowgarth** received the Rea Towing funnel colours in place of the Cory markings seen here. She was eventually despatched for a time to Angola as part of an on-going contract. The **Willowgarth** was, however, normally based on the Mersey, and in 2001 became part of the Wijsmuller fleet when Cory Towage was taken over. In 2006 she is now part of the Svitzer Marine fleet based at Belfast. The **Willowgarth** is propelled by a pair of azimuthing Z-Peller units driven by two 6-cylinder Ruston diesels. She has a bollard pull of 45 tonnes and is fitted for firefighting and pollution control.

(Bob Allen)

The preserved tug **TID 172** is now based near Mistley on the River Stour. She started life in 1946 and was the last TID tug to have been built, although **TID 183** was numerically the last. The first 89 were built as coal burners, whereas **TID 91** to **TID183** had oil-fired boilers. They had a free running speed of up to 8 knots. Unlike many of the TID tugs, she remained in Naval service right through to the early 1970s, based mainly at Chatham Dockyard. She was sold to a breaker on the Thames in July 1973 and the following month bought by a Mr Albert Groom for preservation. In 1975 the **TID 172** moved to Ipswich and was laid up. In 1980 following a plea for help the present group of volunteers took over her restoration. She was steamed in 1981 and has had a lot of work carried out over the years since then. She is normally steamed several weekends each year, and has made the occasional long voyage to places such as Dordrecht in the Netherlands.

(David Dixon)

Alexandra Towing ordered six motor tugs in early 1964. Three of these were to be built by W J Yarwood & Sons at Northwich. The last of this trio was the **Egerton,** which along with the **Langton** and **Brocklebank**, was intended for service at Liverpool. All were powered by a 2-stroke turbocharged Crossley oil engine of 1200bhp. Unlike her sisters, the **Egerton** was moved to Swansea briefly in 1973 to replace a steam tug. She had moved to Felixstowe by December and worked there until her disposal in 1990. The **Egerton** went to new owners in the Dominican Republic as the **Caribe 1**. She is seen proceeding down the River Orwell just below Ipswich docks. Felixstowe-based tugs would often be called upon to provide towage assistance at nearby Ipswich.

(Bernard McCall)

Alexandra Towing's fleet renewal programme in the early 1970s called for a quartet of conventional motor tugs derived from the design of the **Margam** of 1970. All initially entered service at Liverpool in 1972 and the **Crosby** was one of these. The other three were named **Albert**, **Alfred** and **Victoria**. By the early 1980s they were all regularly redeployed elsewhere to ports like Swansea and Southampton. The **Crosby** had a spell at Felixstowe in the 1980s, as seen here in May 1986. Behind the tug are some of the bustling berths that make Felixstowe the busiest container port in the UK. The **Crosby** was sold in 1998 to Portuguese interests and renamed **Montebelo**. In 2000 she was sold to Spanish owners Remolcanosa, of Vigo, who stationed her at Mahon in Menorca.

(Andrew Wiltshire collection)

The **Crested Cock** was very much a classic steam tug. She was a typical Thames based ship-handling tug built at Aberdeen by Alexander Hall in 1935. Her original owners were Gamecock Tugs Ltd, and the **Crested Cock** was the newest of four similar tugs still in service with Gamecock in the post war years. The others were the **Atlantic Cock**, **Ocean Cock** and **Watercock**. They were all equipped with triple expansion steam plant of around 1000ihp. Gamecock Tugs, along with the Wm Watkins and the Elliot fleets, were amalgamated to form Ship Towage Ltd in 1950. However, each company operated its own tugs in its own house colours until 1965 when a new funnel colour was created for all Ship Towage tugs. Her days are nearly over when seen here near Gravesend in May 1969. She is in the colours of Ship Towage Ltd, and was sold for scrap to Belgian breakers in February 1970, after 35 years service.

(Bob Allen)

William Watkins was a long-established London tug owner with its roots going back as far as 1833. Their rather elegant steam tug *Tanga* was built in 1931 by Philip & Son at Dartmouth at a cost of £12,975. She was a development of the *Gondia* and *Kenia* of 1927. The *Tanga* was 106 feet in length, 25 feet in the beam and she had an Earles triple expansion engine of 850ihp. Her early war service took her to Brest in Brittany and other parts of western France and she played a major role in the D-Day evacuation. The *Tanga* then went on to serve in Iceland from 1940. After a refit she returned to the Thames in 1943 and came under the control of Ship Towage Ltd in 1950. The *Tanga* was converted to oil burning in 1958 and was sold to Belgian shipbreakers in 1969. She retained her open wheelhouse throughout. She is seen here on the Thames just off the Royal Docks in 1968.

(C C Beazley)

Two quite good-looking, but very basic tugs were delivered from Richard Dunston at Hessle to Ship Towage Ltd in 1967. The second of these was the *Watercock* and she is seen here in original condition when about 12 months old. The *Watercock* and her sister *Burma* were conventional single-screw tugs of 161 grt and 1050bhp. What was very surprising is that they entered service with a traditional open wheelhouse. This arrangement was obviously not acceptable by the late 1960s, and both were later fitted with an enclosed wheelhouse. The *Watercock* passed to London Tugs and then on to Alexandra Towing in 1975. She remained an active member of Alexandra's Gravesend fleet until 1989 when she was sold for breaking up at Sheerness. The *Watercock* is photographed here in charge of New Zealand Shipping's *Matuara*, also fairly new at the time.

(C C Beazley)

An important historic tug………..and still in steam today. In 2007 the **Challenge** represents steam towage on the Thames over a period four decades, and also played an important role in the D-Day landings of 1940. She was built in 1931 for the Elliott Steam Tug Co, London, by Alexander Hall at Aberdeen. In many respects she was similar to the **Crested Cock** (page 74). The **Challenge** was converted to oil burning as late as 1964 and eventually withdrawn from service with London Tugs Ltd in 1971. As such, she was the last steam tug to serve on the Thames. She is seen here at Gravesend landing stage in 1971 with just months to go. In 1973 the **Challenge** was bought for preservation and put on display at St Katherine's Dock near Tower Bridge. In 1993 she had moved to a berth in Tilbury Docks and was now in the care of the Dunkirk Little Ships Restoration Trust. She was in a very poor state, but restoration began and by 2004 was in full working order. She is now based at Southampton and has regained her flying bridge from her earlier days. She frequently visits maritime festivals.

(C C Beazley)

The **Sun X11** was a development of the **Sun III** (page 69) and was one of 3 similar tugs delivered to Sun Tugs (W H J Alexander) in 1925. As usual they were built by the Earle's Shipbuilding and Engineering Company at Hull and were triple expansion-engined tugs of 183 grt. In this 1969 view we see her in the colours of London Tugs Ltd and passing the Woolwich Ferry. Like so many tugs she was requisitioned during World War 2 and took part in D-Day rescues before being sent to work on the Clyde from 1942 until 1945. Returning to life on the Thames, she was converted to oil burning in 1957. Her last few months in service were in the ownership of London Tugs Ltd. She was sold to a breaker at Antwerp later in 1969.

(C C Beazley)

The **Sun XX** was handed over to W H J Alexander on 19 October 1956. She followed her sistership **Sun XIX** into service. She was a product of Philip and Son Ltd, of Dartmouth, who specialised in building smaller craft including many tugs. The **Sun XX** was a useful size at 192 grt and her Ruston & Hornsby engine had an output of 1200bhp. She was originally certified to carry 77 passengers. She would be followed by a similar but slightly more powerful pair of tugs, **Sun XXI** and **Sun XXII**, in 1959 and 1960. She passed to London Tugs in 1969 and to Alexandra Towing in 1975. The **Sun XX** is seen here approaching the landing stage at Gravesend in 1971 in the colours of London Tugs. In 1979 she was sold along with the **Sun XIX** for further service at Naples and became the **Sole Secondo**. As such she saw 17 years service before being sold for breaking up in Turkey in 1996.

(C C Beazley)

Here we see the Port of London Authority (PLA) owned single unit Voith-Schneider tractor tug **Plasma**. Four of these tugs were delivered between 1965 and 1966 for use in the London dock system, primarily in the Royal Docks and at Tilbury. They followed very closely the design of similar tugs already at work with the port authority at Antwerp in Belgium. The **Plasma** was built by Dunston at Hessle in 1965 and was powered by a 16-cylinder Blackstone engine of 1600bhp, giving her a bollard pull of 16 tonnes. She was 122 grt and 87 feet in length. She became the **Burma** of Alexandra Towing in 1991 based at Gravesend. She came under the control of Howard Smith Towage in 1992. She was moved to Swansea as the **Burma** and became the **Langland** in 1994. Four years later she was moved on again, this time to Grimsby and was renamed **Lady Joan**. She remains at Grimsby in 2006, but privately owned. The **Plasma** is pictured in tranquil conditions out in the River Thames in March 1973.

(Andrew Wiltshire collection)

The **Sun XXVII** was the last vessel to be delivered to W H J Alexander (Sun Tugs) before this company was taken over by London Tugs in 1969. Besides being the last of the line, she was the last tug to be built at Faversham by J Pollock, Sons & Co Ltd. She was a large tug of 226 grt and 116 feet in length. The **Sun XXVII** had a 6-cylinder Mirrlees National diesel with an ouput of 2400bhp. The **Sun XXV11** is seen approaching the landing stage at Gravesend on 21 January 1984 and carries the colours of Alexandra Towing. Alexandra chose to use Gravesend as its main base and office on the Thames, as activities further up the river continued to decline. Subsequently, she passed with the Alexandra Towing business to Howard Smith Towage in 1992 receiving their house livery. She was sold in 1997 along with the earlier **Sun XXV** and **Sun XXVI** to Taipan Shipping, Trinidad, and named **Saga Sun**. By 2003 she was working for H C L Marine in Trinidad.

(Paul Andow)

The **Burma** is the sister tug to the **Watercock** (see page 75). We see her approaching the Royal Terrace Pier at Gravesend on a very sunny but cold 21 January 1984. She now has an enclosed wheelhouse that has blended well with the original woodwork of her previous open arrangement. Her funnel is massive for a motor tug, and acts as a superb advert for the Alexandra Towing colour scheme. Like the **Watercock** she had a bollard pull of 16 tonnes. She was sold for scrap in November 1989 and broken up in a drydock at Sheerness after 22 years service.

(Andrew Wiltshire)

Wm Cory and Son was one of a number of shipping companies which operated a fleet of barge-handling tugs on the Thames. They also had a subsidiary company, The Mercantile Lighterage Ltd, which operated the tug **Hurricane** of 1938. She was built as a motor tug by Henry Scarr at Hessle for James W Cook & Co. Between 1939 and 1946 she worked for the Royal Navy and originally had a 550bhp diesel. This was replaced in 1970 by a 660bhp Lister Blackstone engine. Here she heads downstream with a group of loaded barges on 16 July 1976. The **Hurricane** was sold in 1982 to Braithwaite and Dean. By the late 1990s she had passed to Thames and Medway Towage and by 2004 was lying derelict near Woolwich, later moving to Deptford Creek.

(C C Beazley)

The **G P McCann** has paused on the River Thames opposite the entrance to St Katherine's Dock. Visible in the background is part of Tower Bridge and also the old Courage Anchor Brewhouse. The date is 8 September 1984 and this 28 year old tug started life in 1956 as the **St. Olaf**. She was put to work on the same river for B Jacob & Sons Ltd. By 1965 she had passed to Humphrey and Grey (Lighterage) Ltd, London. The **St. Olaf** was built by P K Harris at Appledore and was 37 grt. She was typical of a 1950s Thames river tug with a 360bhp diesel. She became **G P McCann** in 1980 upon sale to M Tugs Ltd, of London. She then passed to Hampson Marine at Fleetwood as **St Olaf** in the 1990s, and was with a Mr Jones of Reading by 1999.

(John Wiltshire)